How to Survive Being a

TEACHER

CLIVE WHICHELOW *and* **MIKE HASKINS**

summersdale

HOW TO SURVIVE BEING A TEACHER

Summersdale Publishers Ltd
46 West Street
Chichester
West Sussex
PO19 1RP
UK

www.summersdale.com

Printed and bound in China

ISBN: 978-1-78685-253-3

Substantial discounts on bulk quantities of Summersdale books are available to corporations, professional associations and other organisations. For details contact general enquiries: telephone: +44 (0) 1243 771107 or email: enquiries@summersdale.com.

To....................................

From..................................

Introduction

They say that to be a teacher you need dedication. Don't they mean 'medication'?

Being a teacher isn't all jolly hockey sticks and free apples. Some parents might think the school day ends when the last bell goes – but, no, it's only over when the last teacher goes. And where do they go? Straight to the pub? No: home to a pile of marking and lesson-planning for the next day.

But there are upsides too. The light bulb moments when one of the more, er, 'challenging' members of your class suddenly realises that two twos are four (and not little ballet skirts) or that Henry the Eighth is not some sort of posh fraction.

Then there's the camaraderie. Every school is a village, and teachers are members of the ruling class (no pun intended). This village has its own laws and you are a senior judge – or at least a barrister. You are one of the inner circle, a member of the elite in this mini-society and you have a bond with your fellow teachers. Possibly a bond like long-term hostages have, but a bond nevertheless.

In your career you might be sworn at, shouted at, or even spat at... on the other hand you might have a *nice* head teacher.

Don't worry, it's all going to be fine. All you need to do is learn the survival techniques.

TYPES OF TEACHER YOU COULD BE

A Dewey Finn – managing to keep the attention of the class by means of face-melting guitar solos

. . . .

A Miss Jean Brodie – maintaining stern discipline (but only through unfortunate fascist tendencies)

. . . .

A Miss Honey – loved by all, but perhaps adopting one of the children might be a step too far

A PROFESSOR DUMBLEDORE —
GENIAL AND WISE,
BUT, IF A STUDENT
MISBEHAVES,
CAPABLE OF CASTING
A SPELL TO ENCASE
THEIR HEAD IN
A PUMPKIN

HOW PEOPLE WILL KNOW YOU'RE A TEACHER

You make the members of your family line up before they enter your house

. . . .

You threaten people talking in the cinema with detention

. . . .

In restaurants, you walk up and down telling people to stay off their mobiles and keep their elbows in

. . . .

In the event of an emergency you will not only take charge, you will take a register

MISTAKES TO AVOID WHEN IN FRONT OF THE CLASS

Writing on the electronic whiteboard with a magic marker

. . . .

Trying to be too friendly by sending friend requests to all your students on Facebook

. . . .

Addressing the entire lesson to the most dominant student in the class – this is particularly bad if they are off sick

Leaving your mobile phone on – especially if the ringtone is 'Anarchy in the UK'

ESSENTIAL
EQUIPMENT FOR
THE CLASSROOM

Ear defenders for noisy classrooms, and air freshener to combat the effects of students who break wind in class

A smartphone for you to discreetly Google answers to questions you should really know

. . . .

A pack of cheap pencils for students who have forgotten their own writing implements (which you can sell to them at a significant profit)

. . . .

A box of plasters for any students who suffer paper cuts (N.B. Under no circumstances use these to tape disruptive students' mouths shut)

FANTASY AND REALITY OF HOW YOU WILL BE REGARDED AS A TEACHER

FANTASY	REALITY
You will be seen as a beloved and respected elder who really understands young people	You will be seen as an out-of-touch loser whose sole mission is to spoil children's fun
Your class will listen, fascinated, as you instruct them	Your class will look fascinated by what's going on outside of the window as you instruct them
At the end of term, your class will achieve exceptional exam results	At the end of term, your class will achieve exceptional exam results... but not in a good way
You will be someone your class will remember with affection for years to come	You will be someone your class will blame for their poor results for years to come

THINGS YOU ONLY DO WHEN YOU HEAR THE SCHOOL INSPECTORS ARE COMING

Meticulously plan your lesson in advance as though it were a military campaign

. . . .

Double-check that you can remember the names of all the kids in your class

. . . .

Print off reams of data like you've been meaning to do for the past 18 months

. . . .

Bribe your class to behave

BREAKDOWN OF TIME SPENT DURING A LESSON

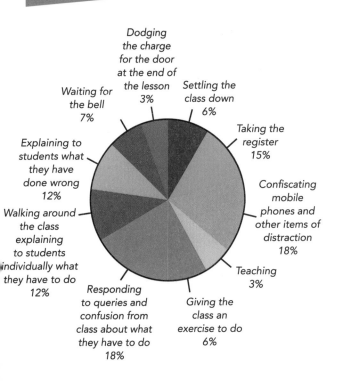

Dodging the charge for the door at the end of the lesson
3%

Waiting for the bell
7%

Explaining to students what they have done wrong
12%

Walking around the class explaining to students individually what they have to do
12%

Responding to queries and confusion from class about what they have to do
18%

Settling the class down
6%

Taking the register
15%

Confiscating mobile phones and other items of distraction
18%

Teaching
3%

Giving the class an exercise to do
6%

OLD-SCHOOL CLASSROOM PUNISHMENTS YOU WISH YOU COULD BRING BACK

The dunce's cap – although the classroom doesn't have enough corners to stand all the little so-and-sos in

The cat-o'-nine-tails – this was probably never a school punishment, but perhaps that's where it all went wrong

• • • • • • • • • •

A wooden bat to dish out six of the best – these days you could really frighten them by threatening to use it to flatten their smartphones

The darkened cupboard inside which misbehaving students could be locked – although you'd often be quite happy to spend the lesson in there yourself

PROFILE OF YOUR IDEAL CLASS AND YOUR CLASS FROM HELL

IDEAL CLASS	CLASS FROM HELL
Keen, eager to learn, and asking intelligent questions	Cantankerous, eager to leave, and questioning your authority
Well-behaved, respectful and punctual	'Well-bored', resentful and punching each other
Diligent, wide-eyed and thirsting for knowledge	Indignant, wild-eyed and thirsting for blood
Resourceful, ambitious and looking bright	Resentful, vicious and looking for a fight

EMOTIONAL RESPONSES YOU SHOULD PRACTISE

Looking as though you are barely
managing to control a volcanic eruption

· · · · · · · · · ·

Appearing morally outraged by behaviour
that you secretly thought was quite funny

· · · · · · · · · ·

Being solemnly cool and collected
like a Wild West gunslinger

LOOKING SHOCKED
AND HORRIFIED AT
THE SORT OF BAD
LANGUAGE YOU
USE AT HOME
ALL THE TIME

HOW TO APPEAR SCARIER THAN YOU REALLY ARE

Grow a big, bad, bristly beard (especially effective if you are a woman)

· · · · · · · · · ·

Bulge your eyes out in a wild, crazy way – although don't do this so much that you make yourself look constipated

· · · · · · · · · ·

Have a box hidden behind your desk that you can stand on and add another 10 inches to your height

Wear a pair of fake vampire-style fangs which you only very occasionally flash to members of the class

GOOD AND BAD WAYS TO END A LESSON

GOOD	BAD
Giving out achievement points to students who have done well	Giving out achievement points to students who have actually bothered to turn up
Summing up what they have learnt and leaving them with something to think about	Totting up the cost of the damage to the classroom and leaving them with the bill
Giving out homework for students to complete before the next lesson	Giving yourself a job application form so you can try to escape before having to teach the little horrors again
Getting students to pack their things away neatly and tidily	Packing yourself away neatly and tidily to avoid the stampede as the students rush for the door

THINGS STUDENTS DON'T WANT TO HEAR FROM TEACHERS

A detailed critical analysis of what you think
is wrong with the national curriculum

. . . .

How they can work hard to
become teachers themselves

. . . .

How difficult you find it surviving
on a teacher's salary

How you find the
latest boy band/grime
artist 'really cool'

DOs AND DON'Ts FOR PARENTS' EVENING

Do try to focus on the positives when discussing students

Don't assure the parents that their semi-feral offspring are future prime ministers-in-waiting

. . . .

Do remind yourself of the students' identities with a sneaky look at their class photo

Don't use their police mugshots

<u>DO</u> HAVE A CLEARLY ORGANISED, WELL PREPARED SET OF NOTES FOR EACH CHILD

<u>DON'T</u> HAVE COMMENTS SUCH AS 'IMBECILE' OR 'COMPLETE NIGHTMARE' IN LARGE, CLEARLY LEGIBLE WRITING

Do make eye contact
and smile

Don't have a fixed rictus
grin that will make the
parents fear for their
children's safety

WAYS TO MAKE DETENTIONS LESS BORING FOR YOURSELF

Mentally play 'whinge bingo' with the various moans and self-justifications of your reluctant captives

. . . .

Make students sit through a long video of your walking holiday in Cumbria

. . . .

Craftily watch a TV show on your smartphone – and keep the detainees longer if they distract you and you have to start again from the beginning

GOOD AND BAD WAYS TO REMEMBER THE NAMES OF PUPILS IN YOUR CLASS

GOOD	BAD
Make up playful word associations that will remind you of each student's name	Make up your own name for each student, such as Spotty McPustule or Stig of the Dump
Learn your students' names by taking the register at the beginning of a lesson	Learn your students' names by taking the register over and over again until the lesson has ended
Call out their names as you hand out their books	Call out their names in the middle of the night as you wake up in a cold sweat
Link their names with their behaviour – 'Stinky Steven', 'Annoying Annie', etc.	Actually call them by these names at parents' evening

WHAT TO DO WHEN STUDENTS SPOT YOU OUTSIDE OF SCHOOL

Change your voice and say you're always getting mistaken for them

. . . .

Try to ignore whatever illegal/ anti-social activities they're engaged in

CHASE THEM AWAY
BY THREATENING
TO DO A BIT OF
IMPROMPTU
REVISION THERE
AND THEN

Really embarrass
them by going over
and hanging out with
them and their friends

THINGS NOT TO SAY TO STUDENTS JUST BEFORE THEIR EXAMS

'Here, borrow my
lucky rabbit's foot –
it's your only hope!'

'Which exam board syllabus
were we studying?'

. . . .

'I've had a sneaky peek at the
exam paper and, sadly, nothing
I've taught you has come up!'

. . . .

'The funny thing is I'm not really
qualified to be a teacher at all!
I just made up everything I
taught you as I went along!'

THINGS YOU SHOULD/SHOULDN'T SAY TO THE HEAD TEACHER

SHOULD SAY	SHOULDN'T SAY
'I'm so glad of your support and trust in me'	'Don't I know you from somewhere?'
'You've done wonders with this school'	'I remember the good old days before you came'
'You have a real vision for the school'	'Unfortunately, it is short-sighted'
'You've really turned this school around'	'It was doing so well before'

ESSENTIAL
ITEMS FOR A TEACHER'S BAG OR BRIEFCASE

A flare gun in case you ever need a way to distract the class or signal for emergency assistance

Headache pills, tranquillisers
and a stress ball

. . . .

A bag of sweets to bribe the
little darlings as a last resort

. . . .

A card showing your blood
group and next of kin

PHRASES TO AVOID WHEN PHONING PARENTS

'Police wanted list'

. . . .

'Little terror'

. . . .

'Legal action may not just be likely but inevitable'

. . . .

'The head teacher's condition is described as critical'

'You do not have to say anything. But, it may harm your defence if you do not mention when questioned something which you later rely on in court'

GIFTS
YOU MIGHT APPRECIATE FROM STUDENTS OR THEIR PARENTS

The return of your car keys which disappeared from your desk at the beginning of term

Pencils with your name
embossed on each one

. . . .

A signed affidavit protecting you from
prosecution if you are goaded into
giving them a clip round the ear

. . . .

A bottle of hard liquor to keep in
your desk drawer for emergencies

THINGS THAT WILL AND WON'T IMPRESS STUDENTS

WON'T IMPRESS THEM	WILL IMPRESS THEM
That you know three languages	That you know three ways to kill someone with a single blow
That you can play the guitar	That you know somebody famous who plays the guitar
You are qualified to teach design	Your shoes have designer labels
You spent four years at university	You spent four years in prison

GIFTS
YOU DEFINITELY WOULDN'T APPRECIATE FROM STUDENTS (OR THEIR PARENTS)

The Dummy's Guide to Effective Teaching

Copies of incriminating photos of
yourself with a demand for money
and/or preferential exam marks

. . . .

Pencils with the obscene nickname
the kids call you behind your
back embossed on each one

. . . .

A can of deodorant and
breath freshener

THINGS YOU SHOULDN'T GIVE DETENTIONS FOR

In order to give yourself some
company when you have to stay late
to catch up on some marking

. . . .

To prevent a student leaving the room
to file a complaint against you

. . . .

Because the student was
'looking at you funny'

Because a student has had a haircut that's so extreme it causes disruption in the class

SELF-HELP BOOKS FOR TEACHERS

A Beginner's Guide to Looking Much More Intimidating Than You Really Are

· · · · · · · · · ·

A Dictionary of Youth-Speak

· · · · · · · · · ·

The Pros and Cons of Voluntary Redundancy

· · · · · · · · · ·

101 Things Students Won't Want to Know About You

DOs AND DON'Ts FOR MAINTAINING DISCIPLINE

DO	DON'T
Give your students positive feedback	Give your students positive electric shocks
Model the behaviour you expect from your students in the classroom	Model a ninja warrior outfit in the classroom
Threaten to contact their parents	Threaten to contact their dead relatives by ouija board
Send them out of the classroom if they are being disruptive	Send the entire class outside so you can have a bit of peace and quiet

INSULTS
FROM STUDENTS AND SUGGESTED RESPONSES

'You're not cool, Miss!' –
'No, since I started
teaching you I've been
boiling with rage!'

'You're past it, sir!' – 'Yes, and I'll tell you what else I've passed – all my exams. Unlike you!'

· · · · · · · · · ·

'Those that can, do; those who can't, teach!' – 'And those who ignore their teachers will end up in the doo-doo!'

· · · · · · · · · ·

'I'll get my dad on you!' – 'Yes, I remember teaching him about twenty years ago!'

THINGS EXPECTED OF YOU NOW YOU'RE A TEACHER

You will know the answer to every single question your students throw at you – haven't they heard of Google?

. . . .

You'll be the living exemplar of politeness and respect – despite doing a job where you may receive no politeness or respect all day

. . . .

That you are also a social worker, policeman, nurse, prison guard and counsellor – unfortunately you still only get the one salary

Not only will you keep a group of potential ruffians under your watchful eye all day, you'll send them home with a passion for Jane Austen, the repeal of the Corn Laws and isosceles triangles

CHANGES THAT WILL OCCUR IN YOUR APPEARANCE

You will become lopsided from carrying
piles of heavy exercise books

. . . .

You will wear disguises outside school
so you can slip into the supermarket/
cinema/pub unnoticed by your students

. . . .

You will have either a stoop or a
cricked neck depending on whether
you are used to regularly speaking
to older or younger pupils

YOU WILL HAVE
PERMANENTLY
PURSED LIPS AND
NARROWED EYES
FROM MAKING
BLOOD-CURDLING
THREATS TO
UNRULY STUDENTS

WAYS IN WHICH FILMS AND TV SHOWS ABOUT SCHOOLS GET IT WRONG

Your class are unlikely to break out into impromptu song and dance numbers

The class are not always listening
with rapt attention to every
word the teacher says

. . . .

The class clown is probably not
going to be regularly coming up
with brilliantly scripted one-liners

. . . .

Your older students will be spotty
children and not, as depicted in
many films, beautifully coiffured
actors in their late twenties

BREAKDOWN OF YOUR EXPENDITURE AS A TEACHER

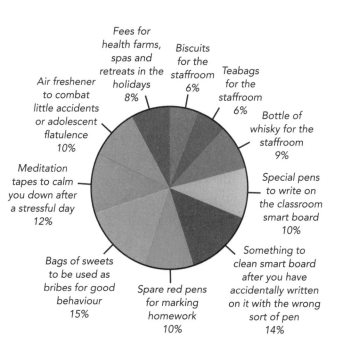

Fees for health farms, spas and retreats in the holidays
8%

Biscuits for the staffroom
6%

Teabags for the staffroom
6%

Bottle of whisky for the staffroom
9%

Special pens to write on the classroom smart board
10%

Something to clean smart board after you have accidentally written on it with the wrong sort of pen
14%

Spare red pens for marking homework
10%

Bags of sweets to be used as bribes for good behaviour
15%

Meditation tapes to calm you down after a stressful day
12%

Air freshener to combat little accidents or adolescent flatulence
10%

WAYS IN WHICH YOU MAY BE TRYING TOO HARD TO LOOK COOL IN FRONT OF THE KIDS

You are the initiator of 'Skateboard to School' week

When you come in one day without your shades and no one recognises you

. . . .

Students complain about the dazzling glare from your extensive array of bling jewellery

. . . .

You decide to get your entire
right arm tattooed – and have it
done in front of the class

REALISTIC AND UNREALISTIC GOALS

REALISTIC	UNREALISTIC
To fill your students with a lifelong passion for learning	To fill your students with a lifelong passion for trigonometry
To equip your students with the skills and intelligence they need for life	To equip your students with the skills they need to create artificial intelligence
Teaching them the importance of personal responsibility	Teaching them the importance of personal hygiene
Helping them achieve some qualifications	Helping them achieve a CBE

THINGS
THAT WON'T ACTUALLY
IMPRESS SCHOOL INSPECTORS

Your 'star pupil' has a beard and is actually another teacher

A clearly pre-prepared and frenetic lesson during which your students make a lasagne, solve Fermat's Last Theorem and isolate the Higg's boson all in 40 minutes

· · · · · · · · · ·

Your students are not only working to a pre-planned script but are reading from an autocue you have set up at the front of the class

· · · · · · · · · ·

Your classroom is neat, tidy and spotless – mainly because you've told all the kids to stay away for the day

ACTIVITIES YOU SHOULDN'T ENGAGE IN WHEN IN FRONT OF THE CLASS

Sharing any grudges you have
against your fellow teachers

. . . .

Ordering in a takeaway because you
don't like the school dinners

. . . .

Swigging from a bottle of booze
to stop yourself shaking

Assuming a yoga
position and meditating
in an effort to make
it all go away

THE TEACHER'S WARDROBE — WHAT TO WEAR AND WHAT NOT TO WEAR

DO WEAR	DON'T WEAR
Something smart to suit your status	Expensive designer outfits that will undermine your 'underpaid public servant' image
Hard-wearing clothes that will withstand spilt drinks, sticky sweets, chewing gum and other occupational hazards	Radiation protection clothing complete with helmet and breathing apparatus
Something casual and comfortable	Your dressing gown and pyjamas
Your finest power-dressing outfit to show your class you are not to be messed with	A Darth Vader costume

WAYS STUDENTS WILL REALISE YOU'RE NEW TO THIS LARK

If you ask them what they would like to study today

. . . .

If you have a panic button installed under your desk

*If you shake hands with
each of them as they
enter the classroom*

THINGS ONLY A TEACHER WOULD FIND EXCITING

The latest developments in interactive whiteboard technology

. . . .

This week's edition of *The Times Educational Supplement* coming through the letter box

. . . .

The day when half the class is going off on a geography field trip

. . . .

It's the last day of term!

ADVANTAGES AND DISADVANTAGES OF BEING A TEACHER

ADVANTAGES	DISADVANTAGES
You will be seen as a pillar of the community, a role model and will be highly respected	But not by your students, of course
You will see some of your students go on to highly paid, successful careers	Some of them, however, will become teachers and may end up as your head of department
You will prepare your students for their lives ahead	Your students will be sure to blame you when their lives go horribly wrong
Your students will always remember you	Your students will remember you by doing a funny impression of you at your funeral

WAYS TO MAKE SCHOOL MORE FUN FOR YOURSELF

Hand the students' books out
with a clay-pigeon launcher

· · · · · · · · · ·

Demand applause at the end of
every sentence you utter

· · · · · · · · · ·

Imagine you're presenting a quiz
show on television and that your
students are the contestants

IMAGINE YOUR STUDENTS ARE USING THE PHONES THEY FIDDLE WITH DURING YOUR LESSON TO TEXT YOUR WISE WORDS TO THEIR FRIENDS

THINGS TO KEEP TELLING YOURSELF

You're the boss – even though it doesn't always feel that way

. . . .

You're doing a valuable job for the community, part of which is keeping some of the biggest troublemakers off the streets

. . . .

Your students will look back and appreciate all you did for them – unfortunately they probably won't appreciate it at the time

YOU'RE PREPARING
YOUR STUDENTS
FOR THE TIME WHEN
THEY HAVE TO LEAVE
THE SCHOOL –
SOMETHING WHICH
HOPEFULLY YOU
WILL NEVER HAVE
TO DO YOURSELF

If you're interested in finding out more about our books, find us on Facebook at **Summersdale Publishers** and follow us on Twitter at **@Summersdale**.

www.summersdale.com